Light bulbs extracted from snake

GAINESVILLE, Fla.—A 4-foot pine snake that swallowed two light bulbs has a bright future now that it's undergone surgery to have the bulbs removed.

A farmer found the unlucky snake with two lumps in its stomach wriggling across his front yard northeast of here Sunday afternoon and immediately knew what the problem was....

From *The Associated Press*

A Snake Mistake
Copyright © 1991 by Mavis Smith
Printed in Singapore. All rights reserved.
Produced by Harriet Ziefert, Inc.
ISBN 0-06-107426-8 (pbk.)
First Paperback Edition, 1991
News article on page one
copyright © 1988 by The Associated Press.
Reprinted by permission.

Library of Congress Cataloging-in-Publication Data
Smith, Mavis.
    A snake mistake / Mavis Smith.
      p.   cm. — (An amazing animal reader!)
    "Based on a true story"—CIP galley.
    Summary: After Farmer Henry uses light bulbs as fake eggs to fool
his hens into laying more eggs, Jake the Snake makes a big mistake.
Includes related activities involving amazing facts about snakes and
other animals.
    ISBN 0-06-026909-X (lib. bdg.). — ISBN 0-06-107426-8 (pbk.)
    [1. Snakes—Fiction.] I. Title. II. Series.
PZ7.S65528Sn 1991   90-43152
[E]—dc20   CIP
                                              AC

An Amazing Animal Reader!

A SNAKE MISTAKE

Mavis Smith

HarperCollins*Publishers*

Farmer Henry was worried. His chickens were not laying enough eggs. So he went to the library and took out a book. "Chickens will lay more eggs if you put fake eggs in their nests," he read.

Now Farmer Henry knew just what to do.
He found a box of old light bulbs. "These bulbs
should make very good fake eggs," he said to himself.

"I hope this works," said Farmer Henry.
"I want eggs—lots of them."

Jake, the snake, wanted eggs too.
He slithered up to the chicken coop.

When the chickens saw Jake,
they went wild!

Jake slithered to the first nest he saw.
He opened his mouth wide and…

gulped down his dinner.

Farmer Henry heard the chickens squawking.
Cluck! Cluck! Cluck-cluck! Cluck-cluck!
He ran out of his house as fast as he could.
And there was Jake—propped against a rock—
and going nowhere.

"You look like one sick snake!"
said Farmer Henry. "But it serves you right.
You shouldn't have been in my chicken coop!"

Farmer Henry put Jake on the ground and started back toward the house.

But he soon turned around. He knew he couldn't let Jake just lie there and suffer. He picked him up and said, "I'll take you to the animal hospital. Maybe the vet will know what to do with you."

Farmer Henry put Jake on the examining table.
The doctors stretched him out.

They took an x-ray.
"Very unusual," said the first doctor.

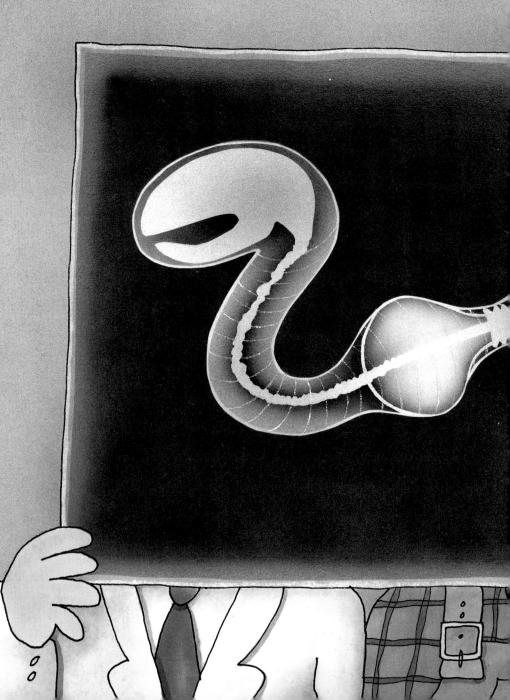

"Hmmm," said the second doctor.
"We must operate right away!"
   they said together.

Farmer Henry waited a long time
outside the operating room.

He read magazines and played cards.
And he thought about Jake.

Finally, a doctor came out.
"Is Jake all right?" Farmer Henry asked.

"He's all right now," said the doctor. "But it's lucky we operated on him before the bulbs broke inside his stomach."

The thought of a stomach full of broken glass made Farmer Henry wince.

Farmer Henry followed the doctor to the recovery room. There was Jake—lying in a special incubator and all hooked up to machines. Farmer Henry was upset.

"I meant to fool the chickens," he said. "But not Jake!"

"Don't worry about him," said the doctor.
"He'll be all right in a few days."

And he was!

The doctors said Jake could leave the hospital.
"He's as good as new," they said.
"And we have a little present for you."

That night Farmer Henry threw a big party to celebrate.

Amazing!

Amazing Animal Activities

1. Find an amazing animal story in a magazine or a newspaper. Ask a librarian or other grown-up for help, if you need it.

2. Tell or write an amazing story about a pet you know. Or make one up! If you like, draw pictures and make your own storybook.

3. There are nearly three thousand different kinds of snakes. How many kinds do you know? Make a list. Then use an encyclopedia or a book about snakes to find the names of ten more.

4. Draw pictures of your favorite snakes from the list. Learn some amazing facts about them. You may even want to make an amazing snake picture book of your own.